A GARDEN OF MY OWN

A Garden of My Own

AN ANTHOLOGY
with Wood Engravings by
Yvonne Skargon

TRAFALGAR SQUARE
PUBLISHING

First published in United States of America in 1996 by
Trafalgar Square Publishing, North Pomfret, Vermont 05053

**Printed in Great Britain by Staples Printers
Rochester, Kent**

ISBN 1 57076 059 4

Library of Congress Catalog Card Number: 96-60073

Typeset in Bulmer

This little book is the product of some years of assiduous engraving, desultory reading and intermittent gardening. Its lack of horticultural rigour will I hope be excused by the engravings. It does not purport to be a literal depiction of my garden; we do not run to peacocks or even to geese. But it is a record of many enjoyable hours spent in the garden of my imagination which, happily, is not all that different from my real garden.

Or rather, from a reality which for the moment has fallen victim to building works. Soon, I am assured, it will all seem to have been worth-while. We shall make a new garden and again be able to say, with Andrew Marvell

> I have a garden of my own
> But so with roses overgrown,
> And Lillies, that you would it guess
> To be a little wilderness

Y. S.
Lavenham, January 1996

9

In memory of Frances
So sad, so fresh, the days that are no more

A

The apple is the symbol of temptation even though the Bible does not actually attribute man's downfall to it. It is likely that the fruit of the proto-*Pyrus* which presumably flourished in the Garden of Eden would have been resistible, even to Oscar Wilde. But no doubt he would have fallen for its aesthetic attributes; as evidently, did Bartholomew Anglicus whose Encyclopedia was one of the earliest printed books containing botanical information.

> Malus the Appyll tree is a tree yt bereth apples and is a grete tree in itself ... And makyth shadowe wythe thicke bowes and branches; and fayr with dyvrs blossomes, and floures of swetnesse and lykynge: with goode fruyte and noble. And is gracious in syght and in taste and vertuous in medecyne ...

In Wagner's *Rheingold* Freia is the keeper of the golden apples which give the Gods eternal youth. When she is sold to the giants Fasolt and Fafner, the Gods are deprived of the apples' magic and immediately their powers begin to wane. A dramatic manifestation of the perils of not following the 'apple a day...' prescription.

ANEMONE

The Anemones ...or Windflowers are so full of variety and so dainty, so pleasant and so delightsome flowers, that the sight of them doth enforce an earnest longing desire in the minds of anyone to be a possessour of some of them at the least, for without all doubt this one kind of flower...is of it selfe alone almost sufficient to furnish a garden with their flowers for almost halfe the year...

JOHN PARKINSON *Paradisi in Sole, Paradisus Terrestris* 1629

They are curious, these great, dark violet anemones. You may pass them on a grey day, or at evening or early morning, and never see them. But as you come along in the full sunshine, they seem to be baying at you with all their throats, baying deep purple into the air. Whereas when they are shut, they have a silkiness and a curved head, like the curve of an umbrella handle and a peculiar outward colourlessness that makes them quite invisible.

D . H . LAWRENCE *Flowery Tuscany*

Another who was a Florist, being very importunat, to have some seeds of a speciall Anemonie for a price they Could not agree on; came one day, as desiring onely to walke in the Garden, having a very long Cloake on (as the Priests & churchme(n) usualy ware) pass'd thro' the Beds of those Flowers then in seede, when observing his time, he so drew the bottome of his Cloake as if spread by the aire, the (glew), to which the seedes do allways stick; that in 2 or 3 turnes aboundance of it stuck to his Cloake; & so taking leave of our F(l)orist, when he came to his house, brushing & pricking off the (glew) & seeds, adhering to them; almost quite rob'd Mr. Morine of that which he asked so much for, which I note for a very ingenios Theft:

JOHN EVELYN Paris 1644

Note how much pleasure I get from anemones. I love their Victorian colours, their green ruffs and how, furry as chestnuts, the blooms gradually open and in so doing turn and arrange themselves in the vase, still retaining their beauty even when almost dead, at every stage of their life delightful.

ALAN BENNETT (not, one would have guessed, one of nature's flora fanciers) *Diary* 20 January 1995

13

B

BEE

Then in some flower's belovèd hut
Each bee as sentinel is shut
And sleeps so too: but, if once stirred,
She runs you through, nor asks the word.

ANDREW MARVELL *Upon Appleton House*

14

We all din'd, at that most obliging & universaly Curious Dr. Wilkin's, at Waddum, who was the first who shew'd me the Transparent Apiaries, which he had built like Castles & Palaces & so ordered them one upon another, as to take the Hony without destroying the Bees; These were adorn'd with variety of Dials, little Statues, Vanes &c: very ornamental, & he was so aboundantly civill, as finding me pleasd with them, to present me one of these Hives, which he had empty, & which his Majestie came on purpose to see & contemplate with much satisfaction.

JOHN EVELYN 13 July 1654

BERGAMOT

A garden favourite both for its showy scarlet flowers and its aromatic fragrance. Even when the darkly coloured leaves have died away, the surface rootlets give off the pleasant smell, reminiscent of the Bergamot Orange, by which *Monarda didyma* has earned its common name 'Bergamot'. Bees delight in its nectar-rich blossoms and it is sometimes known as 'Bee Balm'. Bergamot hybrids, rose-pink, purple and white which these days are often grown are, though sweet, less deliciously scented than the scarlet Bergamot or 'Oswego Tea' originally sent to England in 1744.

BUTTERFLY

A beautiful insect, so named because it first appears in the beginning of the season for butter.

SAMUEL JOHNSON *Dictionary*

But the very greatest curiosity which I esteemed, for being very ingenious and particular, was his collection of all the Sorts of Insects, especialy of Buter flys, of which he had so grete Variety; that the like I had never seene; These he spreads, & so medicates, that no corruption invading them he keepes in drawers, so plac'd that they present you with a most surprizing & delightfull tapissry; besides he shewd me the remarkes he had made of their propagation, which he promisd to publish: some of these, as also of his best flowers, he had caus'd to be painted in miniature by rare hands, & some in oyle:

JOHN EVELYN on Monsieur Morine of Paris April 1644

All of a sudden a large butterfly of the Vanessa tribe whirled high above my head. 'A Red Admiral' I think to myself, but that was no Red Admiral, and with a rapture none but a naturalist can ever know I recognize no other than a Camberwell Beauty. It must have come out of its chrysalis this very morning, for it is strong on the wing and after passing rapidly above my head shows no fancy to settle in the road where I stand but at once disappears over the high wall on the other side. I take my net out of my basket and set it up, so as to be quite prepared in the case of another event of equal importance, but no such chance recurs.

MARGARET FOUNTAINE *Love among the Butterflies* 1892

C

… and I saw at a village called Stratton, I think it was, the first campanula that I ever saw in my life. The main stalk was more than four feet high, and there were four stalks, none of which were less than three feet high.

WILLIAM COBBETT *Rural Rides*

CAT

A domestic animal that catches mice, commonly reckoned by naturalists the lowest order of the leonine species.

SAMUEL JOHNSON *Dictionary*

There is a widely held belief that cats and gardens do not go together. Happily, the Mr McGregors of this world are shewn as the crude materialists that they are by no less than Miss Jekyll herself:

My garden would not be half the pleasure it is to me without the pussies ... They are perfect garden companions. When I am out at work there is sure to be one or other of them close by, lying on my jacket or on a bench if there is one near. When it is Tabby, if there is an empty basket anywhere handy he is certain to get into it ... Like most cats he is devoted to the pretty catmint. It is in several places in the garden. He knows where every plant is and never passes one without stopping to nuzzle and nibble it ...when he has had his first taste he will push himself right down into the middle of the plant and sometimes lie down and roll in it to get all he can of the sweet smell.

GERTRUDE JEKYLL *Children and Gardens* 1908

I am taking that large cat into the country for Waley. He saw it was such a trouble to keep in London. And I really get so much pleasure from having many cats to look at on the lawn. Really they are very like the Russians [ballet dancers]. They move so beautifully ...

DORA CARRINGTON to Lytton Strachey 21 May 1919

CA´TERPILLAR. n.s. [It seems easily deducible from *cates*, food, and *piller*, Fr. to rob; the animal that eats up the the fruits of the earth.]

A worm which, when it gets wings, is sustained by leaves and fruits.

SAMUEL JOHNSON *Dictionary*

... There are caterpillars which infest the cabbages and the Swedish turnip, and some other herbaceous plants. These manifestly proceed from the butterfly; but, unfortunately, they do not make their appearance in little pockets or bags; but you make the first discovery of the honour of the visit that they are paying you by perceiving their gnawings upon the edgings of the leaves of the plants. Let them alone for a little while, and they will go from cabbage to cabbage until there is not a bit of leaf left in the whole patch. They leave you the skeleton of a cabbage, taking away all the flesh, and leaving all the bones; that is to say, the stalk of the cabbages and the ribs of the leaves. These are most mischievous things; they are wholly insensible to the powers of lime; in heat they delight; wet will not injure them; frost is their only destroyer; and many a time have I prayed for winter in order to see an end of the caterpillars.

WILLIAM COBBETT *The English Gardener*

D

DAISY

There is a saying 'When you can put your foot on seven daisies summer is come'. In which case summer in this garden is almost perennial. Like the dandelions, with which they so promiscuously co-habit, the 'day's-eyes' shut at night. Its Latin name 'bellis' may be a corruption of 'bellus' (pretty) which would seem more apt than a correspondence with the Latin word for war. In more innocent times daisy petals were pulled off to the count of 'he loves me, he loves me not'; but as there is usually an odd number of flowerets, the knowing, as Ruskin pointed out, could be reasonably 'sure to end with the confirmation of it'.

DANDELION

'Leontodon' in Greek, 'Dens leonis' in Latin, French 'Dent de Leon' – corrupted to Dandelion in English – and similarly named in many other European languages, the 'lion's teeth' are presumed to be the jagged edges of its leaves. It could equally well refer to the hold that *Taraxacum officinale* can take on lawns and other pre-occupations of the fastidious. Those less meticulously inclined may view with more indulgence the flowers' miniature sunbursts in early spring and which continue almost throughout the year. The ripe seed heads when puffed at by children are supposed – according to the number of puffs required to launch all the parachutes – to tell the time. Meteorologically more certainly, the flowers which are sensitive to light close at dusk and open at dawn and respond directly to the threat of wet weather by retreating into tight buds.

September 1, 1800. The beards of thistle and dandelions flying above the lonely mountains like life, and I saw them thro' the trees skimming the lake like swallows.

S.T. COLERIDGE

A cold dark morning. William chopped wood – I brought it in a basket. A cold wind. Wm slept better, but he thinks he looks ill – he is shaving now. He asks me to set down the story of Barbara Wilkinson's turtle dove. Barbara is an old maid. She had two turtle doves. One of them died, the first year I think. The other bird continued to live alone in its cage for 9 years, but for one whole year it had a companion and daily visitor – a little mouse, that used to come and feed with it; and the dove would caress it, and cower over it with its wings, and make a loving noise to it. The mouse, though it did not testify equal delight in the dove's company, yet it was at perfect ease. The poor mouse disappeared, and the dove was left solitary till its death. It died of a short sickness, and was buried under a tree with funeral ceremony by Barbara and her maidens, and one or two others.

DOROTHY WORDSWORTH *Journal* 30 January 1802

E

EUPHORBIA

Reading about the Euphorbiaceae (Spurges) brings to mind Miss Prism's views on the chapter concerning the fall of the rupee – to be omitted, 'it is too sensational'. And there is no doubt that the milky juices of even our relatively tamed garden varieties can inflict acute discomfort on the unwary and susceptible. Mrs Grieve is dire in her description. 'It is a violent irritant and caustic poison. At the Cape, capsules [of the juice] are used for destroying animals. It may produce delirium'. Even so, intrepid (or insouciant) gardeners find the come-hither winks of *E. Wulfenii* hard to resist and need never take on board that the name 'spurge' derives from the Latin word for expurgate in the medical sense.

EMPEROR MOTH

A palpable misnomer, some might think, in these feminist times. As the female sometimes exceeds three inches in wing-span while the male seldom manages more than two-and-a-half, 'Empress' moth seems more appropriate. But if the large lady, little man relationship reminds one of the art of Donald McGill, both sexes share an intricate beauty of marking and colour that fully justifies the jumbo proportions of the display. The Emperor Moth is found widely in Europe and Northern and Western Asia and is the only one of its kind to be found in Britain. A visitation to one's own garden must be accounted a rare privilege and treat.

EARWIG

This is a most pernicious insect, which feeds on flowers and on fruit, and which, if it congregated like the ant, would actually destroy every thing of this sort. Its favourite flowers are those of the carnation kind. To protect very curious plants against them, the florists put their stages on legs, and surround each leg with a circle of water contained in a dish which is so constructed as to admit the leg through the middle of it, seeing that the earwig is

24

no swimmer. Others make little things of paper like extinguish-ers, and put them on the tops of the sticks to which the carna-tion stalks are tied. The ear-wigs commit their depredations in the night, and they find these extinguishers most delightful retreats from the angry eye of man and from the burning rays of the sun. Take off the extinguishers, however, in the morning, give them a tap over a basin of water, and the enjoyments of the ear-wigs are put to an end at once.

WILLIAM COBBETT   *The English gardener*

Ear-wigs, when small, fly about with ease; but, when full-grown do not attempt to rise; as if their wings were not then adequate to their weight.

This is a mistake; there are two species

GILBERT WHITE   24 September 1767

F

FOXGLOVE

As is so often the case, the derivation and meaning of the name is different from what seems obvious. If foxes had to wear gloves one can hardly think of a more appropriate and elegant mitten; but, it appears, it was originally 'Folksglove', the folk being the fairy-folk who were believed to inhabit the same shady dells and glades as their glovers. The etymologically sceptical – or those who were not brought up on Peter Pan – may care to note that its Norwegian name translates as Foxbell and has nothing to do with fairies, and that there is said to be a northern legend that bad fairies gave the flowers to the fox to wear on his toes to deaden his tread when up to no good. The original Hush Puppies perhaps?

FROGS

… It has been often asserted that young frogs & fish will fall from the clouds in storms & it has often (been) wrongly asserted when the phenomena has sprung from natural causes – I have seen thousands of young frogs crossing a common after a shower but I found that they had left their hiding places & pursued their journeys after the shower began early in the morning early risers may see swarms of young frogs leaving their birth places & emigrating as fast as they can hop to new colonys & as soon as the sun gets strong they hide in the grass as well as they are able to await the approach of night to be able to start again but if in the course of the day showers happen to fall they instantly seize the chance & proceed on their journey till the sun looks out & puts a stop to their travelling again…

JOHN CLARE April 21 1825

Another of his violent dislikes was to frogs, the sight of which animal would put him into a cold sweat, and the same with respect to cats. Great pains were therefore taken to put in his way frogs and cats. At dinner, the day the Grants returned, Mordaunt was in a tolerable good humour until offended by the incessant mirth of the two women; at which he grew crabbed,

27

asking what the devil they were giggling at. From their significant nods and signs to each other, I conjectured some mischief was on foot, though I knew not what, not having been let into the secret.

The meat being removed, pastry succeeded. Mrs Grant, drawing a dish to her, said to Mordaunt who sat next to her, 'Captain Mordaunt, will you allow me to help you to a bit of this tart?' He gruffly answered, 'No, ma'am'; to which she with a broad grin replied, 'Dear! now that's very ill-natured, for you like cherry tart and always eat it, and these are, I understand, the first of the season.' He then said he could help himself, pulling the dish from before her, and began to cut it. The moment he took off a piece of the upper crust, out jumped an immense large frog, followed by two or three of lesser size in succession, as fast as could be. Mordaunt instantly fell back in his chair as if he had been shot. Recovering, however, in a few moments he seized a carving knife that lay before him; and had not Grant, who sat on the other side of him, arrested his raised-up arm, I have not a doubt but he would have stabbed Mrs. Grant.

WILLIAM HICKEY *Memoirs*

FERNS

Fern is one of those plants which have their seed on the back of the leaf so small as to escape the sight. Those who perceived that fern was propagated by semination and yet could never see the seed were much at a loss for a solution of the difficulty; and as wonder always endeavours to augment itself they ascribed to fern-seed many strange properties; some of which the rustick virgins have not yet forgotten or exploded.

SAMUEL JOHNSON

Who the rustic virgins were, how Johnson was acquainted with them, and what it was that they believed is unclear. But both Shakespeare and Ben Jonson refer to the attribute of Fern seed to confer invisibility.

Our first parents, if we credit Milton, (as we must,) were not wholly indebted to the spontaneous growths of their happy garden for their green bowers and mossy seats, but with delicate fingers wove the pliant branches into arches of umbrage, and set alleys of sweet scented herbs before their favourite retreats. Who knows but that a Fernery was one of their choice delights? Few rustic adornment would better have become their sylvan home, where shade and coolness, fragrance and verdure, softened the song of love and the hymn of praise.

SHIRLEY HIBBERD
Rustic Adornments for Homes of Taste 1857

A little far-fetched, perhaps: but ferns deserve to be rescued from the neglect that has overtaken them since Mr. Hibberd so eloquently and successfully promoted them.

G

GEESE

... There was a triumphal procession back to the other room, with Gervaise carrying the goose, arms held out stiff, face streaming with perspiration, beaming and speechless, the women walking behind, also grinning, whilst Nana, bringing up the rear, goggled as she stood on tiptoe to see. When the goose was on the table, huge, golden brown and anointed with gravy, they did not attack it straight away. The whole company were struck dumb with awe and respectful amazement, and comments were exchanged with blinkings of eyes and nodding of heads. 'Lumme, what a bird! What legs! What a breast! ...'

... Now, with their jaws a bit rested and a new gap in their stomachs, they resumed their dinner and fell upon the goose with furious energy. The mere fact of waiting and watching the goose being carved, observed the facetious Boche, had sent the veal and the pork right down into his legs.

It was a grand blow-out, and no mistake! Nobody could ever remember such a just cause for indigestion. Gervaise looked huge as she sat leaning on her elbows eating great lumps of white meat and saying never a word for fear of missing a mouthful, but she was just a bit ashamed in front of Goujet, and vexed to be looking as greedy as a cat.

ÉMILE ZOLA *L'Assommoir*

GOOSEBERRY

At a rather daunting luncheon party our hostess, a lady not to be taken lightly, pronounced as she dispensed the delicious fool, 'Did you know that the French have no word for gooseberry?' I didn't, but I now believe it to be not wholly true. Perhaps it was just a way of remarking on the undeniable disregard the French have for this very English fruit. Caution about the origin of names suggests that, etymologically speaking, *Ribes Grossularia* may not have anything much to do with Geese, but there can be no doubt that the sharpness of gooseberry sauce is a delicious foil to the richness and fattiness of the bird. When the French do deign to acknowledge the fruit it is called 'groseille à maquereau', mackerel currant, in acknowledgment, no doubt, of its compatibility with fatty food.

My goose-berries are still very fine, but are much eaten by the dogs.

GILBERT WHITE   16 August 1785

My great-aunt had a favourite Aberdeen, who, incredible though it may seem, loved ripe gooseberries, He used to sit up, as though he were begging, and eat them and wail aloud every few minutes whenever his nose was pricked.

ELEANOR SINCLAIR RHODE   *The Scented Garden* 1931

GOURD

Gourd is a sort of pumkin; but I know not any use that it is of. If any one wish to cultivate it, out of mere curiosity, the directions will be found under 'Pumpkin'.

WILLIAM COBBETT   *The English Garden*

GREENHOUSE

My dear, I will not let you come till the end of May or beginning of June, because before that time my greenhouse will not be ready to receive us, and it is the only pleasant room belonging to us. When the plants go out we go in. I line it with mats, and spread the floor with mats; and there you shall sit with a bed of mignonette at your side, and a hedge of honeysuckles, roses, and jasmine; and I will make you a bouquet of myrtle every day.

WILLIAM COWPER to Lady Hesketh 9 February 1786

My greenhouse is never so pleasant as when we are just upon the point of being turned out of it. The gentleness of the autumnal suns, and the calmness of this latter season, make it much more agreeable retreat than we ever find it in summer; when, the winds being generally brisk, we cannot cool it by admitting a sufficient quantity of air, without being at the same time incommoded by it. But now I sit with all the windows and the doors wide open, and am regaled with the scent of every flower in a garden as full of flowers as I have known how to make it. We keep no bees, but if I lived in a hive I should hardly hear more of their music. All the bees in the neighbourhood resort to a bed of mignonette, opposite to the window, and pay me for the honey they get out of it by a hum, which, though rather monotonous, is as pleasing to my ear as the whistling of my linnets.

WILLIAM COWPER

H

HELLEBORE

Christmas Rose as it is commonly called is as a name usually optimistic; but *Anemone Pulsatilla* perhaps pre-empted Easter when hellebores are more likely to be at their best. The word hellebore comes from the Greek *elein*, to injure, and *bora*, food. It is poisonous but has some useful medicinal and homeopathic properties. The Greek cowherd Mecampe having discovered that hellebores acted as an effective purgative on his cattle, set up in practice with hellebore as his specific. Fortunately his treatment of King Proteus' daughters, who were under the delusion that they had changed into cows, was successful. One of them was given to him in marriage as a reward. And, rather more enduringly, an alternative name for hellebore was coined – Mecampodium.

Helleborns, Many males, many females. The Helleborns niger, or Christmas rose, has a large beautiful white flower, adorned with a circle of tubular two – lip'd nectaries. After impregnation the flower undergoes a remarkable change, the nectaries drop off, but the white corol remains and gradually becomes quite green. This curious metamorphose of the coral, when the nectaries fall off, seems to shew that the white juices of the coral were before carried to the nectaries, for the purpose of producing honey; because when these nectaries fall off, no more of the white juice is secreted in the coral, but it becomes green, and degenerates into a calyx.

ERASMUS DARWIN *The Botanic Garden* 1790

HEDGEHOG

An animal set with prickles, like thorns in an hedge.
SAMUEL JOHNSON Dictionary

Fine haymaking: hay-carting. Young hedge-hogs are frequently found, four or five in a litter. At five or six days old their spines (which are white) grow stiff enough to wound any body's hands.

They, I see, are born blind, like puppies; have small external ears; & can in part draw their skins down over their faces: but are not able to contract themselves into a ball, as they do for defence when well-grown.

GILBERT WHITE   July 1 1769

HODGE

Hodge was so common a rural name that it became a generic term for a rustic. This begs the question as to why Dr Johnson, that most urban of persons, should have named his cat – 'a very fine cat' – Hodge. But there is no question that the Hodge here depicted was named after Johnson's or that, despite incontrovertible Suffolk origins, his black and white elegance is more reminiscent of Fred Astaire than of any country bumpkin.

I

IRIS

The iris is one of the oldest cultivated plants and is recognizably depicted in bas-relief on the walls of the 'Botanical Chamber' in the temple at Karnak of Thutmosis III, who brought iris plants from Syria to Egypt 3500 years ago. To the ancient Egyptians its sceptre-like form symbolised power and majesty, the three leaves of its blossoms representing faith, wisdom and valour. Such stern connotations are softened by the beauty and variety of colours of the flowers of the genus. Its very name is taken from 'Iris', the goddess of the rainbow. Judicious selection of the many species now in cultivation can provide iris blooms of one sort and another for most of the year and to suit varied growing conditions. Nor is it just a pretty face; the rhizomes of *I. Germanica, I. pallida* and *I. Florentina* still grown commercially in Tuscany, provide the source of orris root, used in the preparation of fine perfumes.

IVY

There seems to be a curious association of ivy with alcohol. It formed the wreath of Bacchus and the ancient practice of binding the brow with ivy leaves to prevent intoxication goes along with its leaves forming the poet's crown – a purpose which has not proved notably effective with many who have worn the wreath. More practically, wood of the ivy, which is very porous, was thought to have the property of filtering water from wine and taverns displayed the sign of an ivy bush to indicate that the wine sold there was unadulterated. Hence the saying, which has long outlived any general understanding of its origin, 'A good wine needs no bush'.

This is where an ancient or large ivy grows in some well-sheltered spot on a wall or church, or on large old trees in a wood, and flowers profusely, and when on a warm bright day in later September or in October all the insects which were not wholly dead revive for a season, and are drawn by the ivy's sweetness from all around to that one spot. There are the late butterflies, and wasps and bees of all kinds, and flies of all sizes and colours – green and steel-blue, and grey and black mottled, in thousands and tens of thousands. They are massed on the clustered blossoms, struggling for a place; the air all about the ivy is swarming with them, flying hither and thither, and the humming sound they produce may be heard fifty yards away like a high wind.

W . H . HUDSON *Hampshire Days*

J

JASMINE

The winter flowering *Jasminum nudiflorum*, is so called because the yellow flowers appear without accompanying leaves. It flowers over a considerable time during the winter depending on its position and the degree of shelter it has. Mrs Earle recommended cutting it and taking it indoors; 'During the last three years I have considerably developed the practice of forcing cut blossoming branches in water, in the little hothouse. Even in December if the weather is wet and bad, the *Jasminum nudiflorum* is far more effective and flowers more in a mass, if treated this way, than left on the plant.'

There is also the sweet smelling white Jasmine that blooms in summer against walls. When grown in pots indoors in winter the scent in an enclosed space can be almost overpowering. Gilbert White found it so in summer from outside his window:

The jasmine, now covered with bloom, is very beautiful.
The jasmine is so sweet that I am obliged to quit my chamber
GILBERT WHITE 17 July 1783

> The jasmine, throwing wide her elegant sweets;
> The deep dark green of whose unvarnish'd leaf
> Makes more conspicuous and illumines more
> The bright profusion of her scatter'd stars.
> WILLIAM COWPER

JONQUIL

Of the Narcissus family, Jonquil are notable for their sweet fragrant flowers which occur several on one stalk. In an enclosed space the scent can be heady to the point of nausea: an attribute shared fortuitously by Jasmine, its companion here. Jonquils share with other narcissi the virtues of ease of cultivation and virtual immunity to the depredations of disease and the attentions of animals and insects. The occasional finding of a gnawed or nibbled bulb testifies either to desperation or inexperience, possibly fatal, on the part of the predator. Crispin Van de Pass in his *Hortus Floridus* depicts the dire fate of a large insect laid low

41

by having chewed a daffodil bulb – and serve it right, too. In earlier times jonquils were called Rush Daffodils for reasons which Gerard explains:

The Rush Daffodill hath long, narrow, and thicke leaues, very smooth and flexible, almost round like Rushes, whereof it tooke his syrname Iuncifolius or Rushie. It springeth vp in the beginning of Ianuarie, at which time also the floures do shoot forth their buds at the top of small rushy stalkes, sometimes two, and often more vpon one stalke, made of six small yellow leaues. The cup or crowne in the middle is likewise yellow, in shape resembling the other daffodills, but smaller, and of a strong sweet smell. The root is bulbed, white within, and couered with a blacke skin or filme.

JOHN GERARD *The Herbal*

K

KINGCUP OR MARSH MARIGOLD

The marsh marigold *Caltha palustris* has, it must be said, nothing to do with the common marigold *Calendula officinalis*, being of a completely different natural order. Confusingly, however, the Common Marigold's name is a corruption from the Anglo-Saxon *merso-imeargella*, (marsh marigold), while the

Marsh Marigold's name derives from its use in medieval church festivals as a flower devoted to the Virgin and by reference to its natural habitat in marshes and by streams. Be that as it may, the name Kingcup is wholly apt for this king-size relative of the Buttercup. Shakespeare observes 'winking Marybuds begin to ope their golden eyes' while Chatterton rather more arcanely observes 'The Kingcup brasted with the morning dew'.

KINGFISHER

[A proof of] the severity of the winter, – the kingfisher [by] its slow, short flight permitting you to observe all its colours, almost as if it had been a flower.

S. T. COLERIDGE *Anima Poeta* 1799

This was the most intelligent boy I have met in Hampshire; he knew every bird and almost every insect I spoke to him about. He was, too, a mighty hunter of little birds, and had captured stock doves and wheatears in the rabbit burrows. But his greatest feat was the capture of a kingfisher. He was down by the river with a sparrow-net at a spot where the bushes grow thick and close to the water, when he saw a kingfisher come and alight on a dead twig within three yards of him. The bird had not seen him standing behind the bush: it sat for a few moments on the twig, its eyes fixed on the water, then it dropped swiftly down, and he jumped out and threw the net over it just as it rose up with a minnow in its beak. He took it home and put it in a cage.

I gave him a sharp lecture on the cruelty of caging kingfishers, telling him how senseless it was to confine such a bird, and how impossible to keep it alive in prison. It was better to kill them at once if he wanted to destroy them. 'Of course your kingfisher died,' I said.

'No', he replied. He stood the cage on a chair, and the bird was no sooner in it that his little sister, a child of two who was fidgeting round, pulled open the door and out flew the kingfisher.

W. H. HUDSON *Hampshire Days*

KITTENS

Next morning, to my delight, I saw two very shy little faces peeping out of some garden shrubs and garden plants that were opposite my sitting room window, with only a narrow strip of grass between. As soon as I had finished my breakfast I went out to try and make friends, but the kittens were very wild; they had never been tamed or handled. There was a Dahlia just in front of my window at the edge of the bushes. One of its branches stuck out a little, and to this I tied a string with a bit of white paper fastened in the end, so that it swung about. Then I went in and watched. Presently the darker and more handsomely marked of the two little brothers (my future Tittlebay) came out very cautiously and examined the strange object. It moved and he made a dart at it, which made it swing still further. He soon found out that it was a capital thing to play with. Then his brother came too, and they had a great game. Next morning at breakfast I poured a little milk into a saucer and put it on the grass near the plaything. They came to it by little cautious advances, and lapped up the milk while I stood within sight at the open window. Then I made another plaything, the same as the Dahlia one, only on a stick, like a fishing rod, so that I could play it from the window. After a little hesitation they came to play with it. This was a grand step, because they saw me at the window all the time. Next I put a saucer of milk on the window-sill, and great was my pleasure when Tittlebat came to it. He was the big-

45

ger and stronger of the two, and always took the lead. The next thing was to have the milk on a table put close to the window inside the room.

They came up and on to the table. This was a great advance, and while they were lapping I just stroked them a little, very gently, taking care to bring my hand near them very slowly. A quick movement would have frightened them. Then I knew I had got their confidence. I think this was about five days after the first offer of friendship. Then I pretended to take no notice of them, and the next day they came up to the window of their own accord. Before my fortnight was over Tittlebat came to me as a regular thing, sitting on my lap or my shoulder and purring me his little song while I read or worked. You may imagine that when I went away I could not bear to leave him, so I begged to have him and took him home with me, where I at once gave him into the charge of Pinkie, a young pussy of my own rearing only a few months older. They took to each other at once, and very soon became quite inseparable; in fact, if they were every apart Pinkie was miserable, and would cry most lamentably, looking about for his dear companion.

GERTRUDE JEKYLL *Children and Gardens*

L

LILY

Solomon may come out rather badly from comparison with the genus *Liliaciae* but in his other attribute, wisdom, he certainly puts Lily – a feline definition of flibbertigibbet – in the shade. Why 'Lily'? you may ask. Well, like Hodge (q.v.) she was named after one of Samuel Johnson's cats. But what we overlooked was that his cat was called Lily because she was a '*white* kitling'. We have subsequently thought of re-inventing her name as an abbreviation of 'Tiger-lily', which would at least acknowledge her stripey markings, predatory instincts (even towards lady-birds) and a tendency to return the garden to the state of jungle. But the derivation would be specious and we have long learnt to live with our misnaming of a delightful, destructive and most affectionate f(r)iend.

THE LILY

'O Tiger-lily!' said Alice, addressing herself to one that was waving gracefully about in the wind, 'I wish you could talk!'

'We can talk', said the Tiger-lily, 'When there's anybody worth talking to.'

Alice was so astonished that she couldn't speak for a minute: it quite seemed to take her breath away. At length, as the Tiger-lily only went on waving about, she spoke again, in a timid voice – almost in a whisper. 'And can all the flowers talk?'

'As well as you can,' said the Tiger-lily. 'And a great deal louder.'

'It isn't manners for us to begin, you know,' said the Rose,'and I really was wondering when you would speak. Said I to myself, 'Her face has got some sense in it, though its not a clever one.' Still, you're the right colour, and that goes a long way.'

'I don't care about the colour,' the Tiger-lily remarked. 'If only her petals curled up a little more, she'd be all right.'

LEWIS CARROLL   *Through the Looking Glass*

The modest rose puts forth a thorn:
The humble sheep, a threatening horn:
While the Lilly white shall in Love delight,
Nor a thorn nor a threat stain her beauty bright.

WILLIAM BLAKE
Songs of Innocence and of Experience

M

MAGNOLIA

Named after Pierre Magnol, a renowned professor of botany at Montpelier in the early 18th century, *Magnolia Soulangeanna* is a splendid example of its kind. In the spring before the tree is fully in leaf but showing that it intends to have leaves, the great cup-shaped flowers appear, usually of an ivory-white colour, but subject to be tinged with pink on the outside of the petals. It needs to be grown in a sheltered position as wind and frost turn these beautiful flowers brown.

At Kew yesterday the magnolias were a most melancholy sight; the great pinkish buds just ready to burst into the most magnificent of flowers, & now browned & shrivelled never to open, & while they live to be ugly.

VIRGINIA WOOLF   21 April 1918

MAGPIE

This beautiful bird is everywhere common in England; it is likewise found in various parts of the continent. It feeds like the crow, on almost everything animal as well as vegetable. The female builds her nest with great art, leaving a hole in the side for admittance, and covering the whole upper part with an interweaving of thorny twigs, closely entangled, thereby securing her retreat from the rude attacks of other birds: but it is not safety alone she consults; the inside is furnished with a sort of mattress, composed of wool and other soft materials; on which her young repose: she lays seven or eight eggs, of a pale green colour spotted with black.

THOMAS BEWICK'S   *Birds*

MICE

Here, I confess to cheating. There can never be harvest mice in the garden. But I can find nothing much to say in favour of mice in general and Gilbert White's description of his discovery is as neat and endearing as his subject:

I have procured some of the mice mentioned in my former letters, a young one and a female with young, both of which I have preserved in brandy. From the colour, shape, size, and manner of nesting, I make no doubt but that the species is non-descript. They are much smaller, and more slender, than the *mus domesticus medius* of Ray; and have more of the squirrel or dormouse colour: their belly is white; a straight line along their sides divides the shades of their back and belly. They never enter into houses; are carried into ricks and barns with the sheaves; abound in harvest; and build their nests amidst the straws of the corn above the ground, and sometimes in thistles. They breed as many as eight at a litter, in a little round nest composed of the blades of grass or wheat.

One of these nests I procured this autumn, most artificially platted, and composed of blades of wheat; perfectly round, and about the size of a cricket-ball; with the aperture so ingeniously closed, that there was no discovering to what part it belonged. It was so compact and well filled, that it would roll across the table without being discomposed, though it contained eight little mice that were naked and blind.

GILBERT WHITE to Thomas Pennant 4 November 1767

NASTURTIUM

Nasturtiums & other Indian flowers still in bloom: a sure token
that there has been no frost.

GILBERT WHITE   11 November 1772

An annual plant, with a half-red half-yellow flower, which has an offensive smell; but it bears a seed enveloped in a fleshy pod, taken before the seed becomes ripe, is used as a thing to pickle.

WILLIAM COBBETT *The English Garden*

NUTS

My Brother's turkies avail themselves much of the beech-mast which they find in his grove: they also delight in acorns, wall-nuts, & hasel-nuts: no wonder therefore that they subsist wild in the woods of America, where they are supposed to be indigenous. They swallow hasel-nuts whole.

GILBERT WHITE 1 November 1776

At Blunsdon I saw a clump, or, rather, a sort of orchard, of as fine walnut trees as I ever beheld, and loaded with walnuts. Indeed I have seen great crops of walnuts all the way from London.

WILLIAM COBBETT *Rural Rides*

There is something nutty in the short autumn day – shorter than its duration as measured by hours, for the enjoyable day is between the clearing of the mist and the darkening of the shadows. The nuts are ripe, and with them is associated wine and fruit. They are hard but tasteful; if you eat one you want ten, and after ten twenty. In the wine there is a glow, a pot like tawny sunlight; it falls on your hand as you lift the glass.

They are never really nuts unless you gather them yourself. Put down the gun a minute or two, and pull the boughs this way. One or two may drop of themselves as the branch is shaken, one among brambles, another outwards into the stubble. The leaves rustle against hat and shoulders; a thistle is crushed underfoot, and the down at last released. Bits of bryony hold the ankles, and hazel boughs are stiff and not ready to bend to the will. This

54

large brown nut must be cracked at once; the film slips off the kernel, which is white underneath. It is sweet.

RICHARD JEFFERIES *Nature near London*

The filberd tree that is planted in Orchards, is very like vnto the Hasell nut tree that groweth wilde in the woods, growing vpright, parted into many boughes and tough plyable twigges, without knots, couered with a brownish, speckled, smooth, thinne rinde, and green vnderneath: the leaues are broad, large, wrinkled, and full of veines, cut in on the edges into deepe dents, but not into any gashes, of a dark green colour on the vpperside, and of a grayish ash colour vnderneath: it hath small and long catkins in stead of flowers, that come forth in the Winter, when as they are firme and close, and in the Spring open themselves somewat more, growing longe, and of a brownish yellow colour: the nuts come not vpon those stalkes that bore those catkins, but by themselues, and are wholly inclosed in long, thicke, rough huskes, bearded as it were at the vpper ends, or cut into diuers long iagges, much more then the woodnut: the nut had a thinne and somewhat hard shell, but not so thicke and hard as the woodnut, in some longer then in other, and in the long kinde, one hath the skinne white that couereth the kernals, and another red.

JOHN PARKINSON *Paradisi in Soli* 1629

O

ORANGES

… my Lord Brooke's, where the gardens are much better, but the house not so good, nor the prospect good at all but the gardens are excellent; and here I first saw oranges grow, some green, some half, some a quarter, and some full ripe on the same tree, and one fruit of the same tree doth come a year or two after the other. I pulled off a little one by stealth (the man being

56

mighty curious of them) and eat it; and it was just as other little green small oranges are; as big as half the end of my little finger.

SAMUEL PEPYS   25 June 1666

I remember an occasion at lunch when all the plates were changed and everybody except me was given an orange. I was not allowed an orange as there was an unalterable conviction that fruit is bad for children. I knew I must not ask for one as that would be impertinent. But as I had been given a plate I did venture to say, 'a plate and nothing on it'. Everybody laughed, but I did not get an orange.

BERTRAND RUSSELL   *Autobiography*

Count Ulmarini more famous for his Gardens... especially his Cedrario or Conserve of Organges, Eleaven-score of my Paces long, set in exquisite order & ranges, & making a Canopie all the Way by their intermixing branches, for above 200 of my single paces, & which being full of fruite & blossomes, was one of the most delicious sights, that in my life I had seene.

JOHN EVELYN   April/May 1646

ORCHID

Definitely not a garden plant in England *Orchis Cymbidium* can yet benefit from exposure to the air of fine summer days when, like some exotic beauty at a garden fête, it will attract the admiration of those whose primary interests are not, probably, horticultural. Oranges too require the winter comfort of a heated conservatory – in earlier times a manifestation of wealth and taste; now, more likely, a monument to the powers of persuasion of the double-glazing industry.

P

Pæonies were in ancient times thought to be of divine origin, emanating from the moon and possessed of a luminosity which protected shepherds and their flocks, drove away evil spirits and diverted tempests. They also healed wounds. Later, the pæony acquired more sinister characteristics. 'To pluck it up by the roots will cause danger to he that touches it, therefore a string must be fastened to it in the night and a hungry dog tied thereto, who being allured by the smell of roasted flesh set towards him may pluck it up by the roots.' This had to be done at night 'for if any man shall pluck of the fruit in the daytime, being seen of the woodpecker, he is in danger to lose his eyes.' Gerard who reports these beliefs was sceptical. 'But all these things be most vaine and frivolous, for the root of the Peionne may be removed at any time of the yeare, day, or houre whatsoever.' Even so, it is a plant which does not take kindly to being disturbed and its seeds can take five years or more to germinate. Not on the whole for the impatient.

PEACOCK

Happening to make a visit to my neighbour's peacocks, I could not help observing that the trains of those magnificent birds appear by no means to be their tails; those long feathers growing not from their uropygium, but all up their backs. A range of short brown stiff feathers, about six inches long, fixed in the uropygium, is the real tail, and serves as the fulcrum to prop the train, which is long and top-heavy, when set on end. When the train is up, nothing appears of the bird before but its head and neck; but this would not be the case were those long feathers fixed only in the rump, as may be seen by the turkey-cock when in a strutting attitude. By a strong muscular vibration these birds can make the shafts of their long feathers clatter like the swords of a sword-dancer; then they trample very quick with their feet, and run backwards towards the females.

GILBERT WHITE to Thomas Pennant 1771

59

'Look, look.' cried someone. 'Come and look at the peacock.' We ran to the door and there was the peacock in his pride with his train erected and fully spread, full of great eyes, while the quills rattled and shook with a harsh dry rustle like dead reeds in a wind. 'Ah,' said his mistress, 'that is his pride.' His master, the deaf farmer, came out with some peas and the peacock ate out of his hand and mine. Then the bird began to walk backwards rustling his quills with his train still outspread. 'He walks backwards,' explained his mistress as the bird kept on backing, rattling and rustling his quills, 'because he is so proud. He is a very proud bird.' Then she excused the raggedness of one side of his train by saying the farm lads had pulled the feathers out to stick in their hats o' Sundays.

FRANCIS KILVERT 17 May 1876

Q

QUINCE

These days much neglected the Quince was once a common and valued fruit. One can only think that this was because there were not too many alternatives available. Admittedly the pear-shaped variety is said to be the least congenial of the three principal varieties to be found in Britain; even so it has its followers for making marmalade and for adding piquancy to apple-tarts. The name is said to derive, rather tortuously, from Kydonia the ancient name of Chania in Crete – whose native quinces are the very different, dulcet fruit which, being dedicated to Venus, were regarded as the symbol of Love and Happiness. While no aphrodisiacal properties are associated with it, it is clear that the colour, scent and texture of a ripe quince was capable of arousing delectable sensations in an arab poet of the first century, translated by A.L. Lloyd and quoted by Geoffrey Grigson.

> It has a cloak of ash coloured down hovering over
> its smooth golden body,
> And when it lay naked in my hand, with nothing more
>   than
> its daffodil-covered shift,
> it made me think of her I cannot mention, and I feared
> the ardour of my breath would shrivel it in my fingers.

I think you would have to be deep into heavy leather to get much of that sort of thing from our quinces.

The Quince tree groweth oftentimes to the height and bignesse of a good Apple tree, but more vsually lower, with crooked and spreading armes and branches farre abroad, the leaues are somewhat round, and like the leaues of the Apple tree, but thicker, harder, fuller of veines, and white on the vnderside: the blossomes or flowers are white, now and than dasht ouer with blush, being large and open, like vnto a single Rose: the fruit followeth, which when it is ripe is yellow, and couered with a white cotton or freeze, which in the younger is thicker andmore plentifull, but waxeth lesse and lesse, as the fruit ripeneth, being bunched out many times in seuerall places, and round especially about the head, some greater, others smaller, some round like an Apple, others long like a Peare, of a strong heady sent, accounted not wholesome or long to be endured, and of no durabilitie to keepe, in the middle whereof is a core, with many blackish seedes or kernals therein, lying close together in cels, and compassed with a kind of cleare gelly, which is easier seene in the scalded fruit, then in the raw.

JOHN PARKINSON *Paradisi in Sole* 1629

QUEEN BEE

The Queen-Bee is a faire and stately creature, longer by the half, and much bigger than a common Honey-Bee, yet not so big as a Drone, but somewhat longer. She differs from the common-Bee both in shape and colour; her back is all over of a bright brown, her belly even from the top of her fangs to the tip of her train is clear, beautifull, and of a sad yellow, somewhat deeper than the richest gold: Her head is more round than the little Bees, by reason her fangs bee shorter, her tongue is not half so long as theirs, and thereby nature hath disabled her for working, for it is impossible for her short tongue to extract much out of any flower, were shee never so industrious.

Her wings are of the same size with an ordinary Bees, and therefore in respect of her long body, they seem very short, resembling rather a cloak than a gown, for they reach but to the middle of her train, or nether part. Shee hath streighter, and stronger legs and thighs than a Honey-Bee, which are of the colour of their belly, but her two hind-legs more yellow. Shee hath a lofty pace and countenance expressing Majesty: That shee hath a white spot in her fore-head glistering like a Diadem,

I never saw, though it bee frequently reported: Nay I am sure of the contrary.

The spear of sting shee hath is but little, and not half so long as the other Bees, which, like a Kings sword, is rather born for shew and authority than any other use. I beleeve they cannot use their sting, for I have provoked and forced them to sting by hard holding of them, and putting their taile to my bare hand, but could never perceive them willing to put it forth. Nay when I have forced it out yet shee would not enter it in my hand.

In a word, the Queen Bee in her whole shape and colour, is a goodly and beautiful creature. As the Moon when in a clear night, shee fills her circle, is more and more eminently beautiful than all the lesser stars, so is the Queen Bee among the other Bees.

SAMUEL PURCHAS *A Theatre of Political Flying-Insects* 1657

R

RABBITS

In the case of the rabbits and of the small rodents, we see that they recognize the dangerous character of their pursuer and try their best to escape from him, but that they cannot attain their normal speed – they cannot run as they do from a man, or dog, or other enemy, or as they run ordinarily when chasing one another. Yet it is plain to any one who has watched a rabbit followed by a stoat that they strain every nerve to escape, and, conscious of their weakness, are on the brink of despair and ready to collapse. The rabbit's appearance when he is being followed, even when his foe is at a distance behind, his trembling frame, little hopping movements, and agonizing cries, which may be heard distinctly three or four hundred yards away, remind us of our own state in a bad dream, when some terrible enemy, or some nameless horror, is coming swiftly upon us; when we must put forth our utmost speed to escape instant destruction, yet have a leaden weight on our limbs that prevents us from moving.

W. H. HUDSON *Hampshire Days*

Rabbits make incomparably the finest turf, for they not only bite closer than larger quadrupeds; but they allow no bents to rise: hence warrens produce much the most delicate turf for gardens...

GILBERT WHITE 17 August 1775

Don't go into Mr McGregor's garden: your Father had an accident there; he was put in a pie by Mrs McGregor.

... But Peter who was very naughty ran straight to Mr McGregor's garden and squeezed under the gate.

First he ate some lettuces and some French beans; and then he ate some radishes; and then feeling rather sick he went to look for some parsley.

BEATRIX POTTER *The Tale of Peter Rabbit*

Rhubarb is not to everyone's taste. Significantly, it appears that the use of its stems stewed and in pies and tarts dates only from the late 19th century – the heyday of the nanny and of nursery food. Perhaps it was seen as a slightly more palatable way of fulfilling their duty to ensure that their charges' bowels were kept open. Rhubarb was first introduced from Central Asia for medicinal use as an aperient 'effecting a brisk, healthy purge, without clogging', as Mrs Grieve has it. It was commercially cultivated for its root from about the end of the eighteenth century when men dressed up as Turks were despatched from Banbury in Oxfordshire to sell as genuine rhubarb a concoction made up by an enterprising local apothecary. The deception, if any, lay – then as now – in the marketing rather than in the product, which is said to have been excellent. Nowadays we eat rhubarb, if at all, at the end of winter as a harbinger, perhaps, of better things to come. Whether it is worth the effort of manuring and forcing under large pots, pensioned-off buckets or boxes is perhaps a question. The leaves are toxic and quite recently a cookery book had to be speedily withdrawn when it was discovered to give a recipe for cooking them.

S

SNAILS

Soft rain all days. Snails come forth in troops…
GILBERT WHITE 11 June 1783

The instinct of the snail is very remarkable & worthy notice tho
such things are lookd over with a careless eye – it has such a
knowledge of its own speed that it can get home to a moment to

be safe from the sun as a moment too late would be its death – as soon as the sun has lost its power to hurt in the evening it leaves its hiding place in search of food which it is generally aware were to find if it is a good way off it makes no stoppages in the road but appears to be in great haste & when it has divided its time to the utmost by travelling to such a length as will occupy all the rest of its spare time to return its instinct will suddenly stop & feed on what it finds there & if it finds nothing it will go no further but return homewards & feed on what it chances to meet with & if after it gets home should chance to be under a cloud it will potter about its door way to seek food but it goes no futher & is ready to hide when the sun looks out – when they find any food which suits them they will feed on it till it lasts & travel to this same spot as accurately as if they knew geography or was guided by a mariners compass – the power of instinct in the most trifling insect is very remarkable & displays the omnipotence of its maker in an illustrious manner.

JOHN CLARE   7 February 1825

John Bunyan expresses a similarly indulgent, and not too moralistic view of the snail:

> She goes but softly, but she goeth sure,
> She stumbles not as stronger creatures do;
> Her journey's shorter, so she may endure
> Better than they which do much further go.
>
> She makes no noise, but stilly siezeth on
> The flower or herb appointed for her good,
> The which she quietly doth feed upon,
> While others range and gare but find no good.

69

And though she doth but very softly go,
However 'tis not fast, nor slow, but sure;
And certainly they that do travel so,
The prize they do aim at, they do procure.

[Lord Emsworth] was humming as he approached the terrace. He had his programme all mapped out. For perhaps an hour, till the day had cooled off a little, he would read a pig book in the library. After that he would go and take a sniff at a rose or two and possibly do a bit of snailing. These mild pleasures were all his simple soul demanded. He wanted nothing more.

P. G. WODEHOUSE *Lord Emsworth and Others*

SUNFLOWERS

The Sunflower was only introduced to England in the sixteenth century and there is perhaps an air of wonderment still in Thomas Hyll's description in his *Gardeners Labyrinth* (1577): 'Flowers of the sun groweth very high, and beareth a great yellow flower as big as the crown of a hat…'. Native to Mexico and Peru, the plant appears to have had no difficulty in adapting to northern climates where its value as a source of edible oil and nutriments for humans and livestock was quickly recognised. In Britain it has never been as widely cropped as in other European countries though, courtesy of Brussels, the prairie lands of East Anglia are now occasionally enlivened by serious plantings of *Helianthus annus*. As a garden cultivar it has its drawbacks, not least the requirement in all but the smaller varieties for scaffolding to keep it standing; though its dismissal by Cobbett as 'Fit for nothing but very extensive shrubberies, where seen from a

70

distance, the sight may endure it', is harsh. The Aztecs reverenced it and it formed a central motif of their jewelery and ceremony: five hundred years later it became an icon for the Aesthetic movement. The ubiquity of Van Gogh's sunflowers has not enhanced its reputation.

SWIFTS

At some certain times in the summer I had remarked that swifts were hawking very low for hours together over pools and streams; and could not help inquiring into the object of their pursuit that induced them to descend so much below their usual range. After some trouble, I found that they were taking phryganaea, ephemerae, and libellulae (cadew-flies, may-flies, and dragon-flies) that were just emerged out of their aurelia state. I then no longer wondered that they should be so willing to stoop for a prey that afforded them such plentiful and succulent nourishment.

GILBERT WHITE to Thomas Pennant 28 September 1774

I saw two swifts, entangled with each other, fall out of their nest to the ground from whence they soon rose & flew away. This accident was probably owing to amorous dalliance…

GILBERT WHITE 14 June 1776

T

TORTOISE

Brought away Mrs Snookes' old tortoise, Timothy, which she valued much, & had treated kindly for near 40 years. When dug out of its hibernaculum, it resented the insult by hissing.
GILBERT WHITE *Journal* 17 March 1780

We took the tortoise out of its box, & buried it in the garden: but the weather being warm it heaved up the mould, & walked twice down to the bottom of the long walk to survey the premises.

20 March 1780

Tortoise marches about: eat part of a piece of cucumber paring.

2 May 1780

Tortoise goes under ground: over him is thrown a coat of moss. The border being very light & mellow, the tortoise has thrown the mould entirely over his shell, leaving only a small breathing hole near his head. Timothy lies in the border under the fruit-wall; in an aspect where he will enjoy the warmth of the sun, & where no wet can annoy him: a hen-coop over his back protects him from dogs, &c.

13 November 1780

The tortoise took his usual ramble, & could not be confined within the limits of the garden. His pursuits, which seem to be of the amorous kind, transport him beyond the bounds of his usual gravity at this season. He was missing for some days, but found at last near the upper malt house.

5 June 1787

Timothy the tortoise, who has spent the last two months amidst the umbragious forests of the asparagus-beds, begins now to be sensible of the chilly autumnal mornings; & therefore suns himself under the laurel-hedge, into which he retires at night. He is become sluggish, & does not seem to take any food.

26 August 1787

In the seraglio of the shadow of God, when the world was a few centuries younger, there was one festival in early spring which for dazzling splendour out-shon the rest of the Eastern fairlylike night scenes. Unnumbered articial suns, moons, and stars lit up the Sultan's beautiful gardens, and in the mystic light which turned night into day tens of thousands of Tulips stood proudly up on their tall slim stalks, the goblet of each blossom perfect in form and in colour. Among this dazzling dream the Sultan and his harem, and whoever else was great and mighty at the Court of Constantinople, worshipped at the shrine of the Tulip, and the whole of the East echoed the praise of the thouliban, or turban flower, the corruption of which term has become our name for the flower.

MRS C.W. EARLE *More Pot-Pourri* 1899

We went thence to Monsieur Morines Garden, who from an ordinary Labourer, in that profession, arrived to be not onely a most Extraordinary Florist, but so greate a Vertuoso, that his Collection of Shells, Insects & other natural Curiositys emulats the most famous in Paris, ... Nor lesse Extraordinary was his Garden in forme of an Exact Ovall planted with very talle Cypresse, cut very Even, & with Nices of the same for heads & statues, besides the Parterrs, of the richest Tulips, Anemonies, Ranunculus, Crocus's, Polyants, that could any where be seene, & selling some of them at greate prices; This Constantly drew all the Curiosos of the Towne, & Persons of the highest quality to him, who himselfe liv'd in a kind of Hermitage at one side of his Garden: Two pleasant Storys are not to be forgotten, which concerne his Flowers, the first of two or 3 Tulip bulbs reckoned to be valued at 100 pistoles; which he having wrap'd in a paper, and left upon the Table in his house, a Stranger comming in, with his friend to Visite the old man, & finding no body in the roome, taking the rootes to be but a kind of Onion, Eate them up; one may imagine what rage Morine was in, at the losse.

JOHN EVELYN in Paris, 1644

U

UMBELLIFERAE

There is just one more of the important families of plants that you will very soon learn to recognise. They are called the umbelliferae. You will see more of them in the hedges than in the garden, but if there is a big bog-garden at your home I daresay there will be plants of the giant cow-parsnip, the biggest of the umbel-liferous things. All the Parsley-Carrot-Fennel sort of plants have their flowers in umbels. The flowers in themselves are generally tiny, and mostly white and yellow. They are on a number of little stalks that all branch away from one point on the top of a larger stalk, so that sometimes they make a roundish head and some-times a flat one, or anything between. You may always know the flower of the wild Carrot by its having in the middle of its head of white flowers one little one of a chocolate-red colour.

GERTRUDE JEKYLL *Children and Gardens* 1908

UNICORN

A beast, whether real or fabulous, that only has one horn.

SAMUEL JOHNSON *Dictionary*

A definition which seems to suggest that even the great lexicog-rapher was at least open to the belief that the unicorn could be real.

Our first encounters with unicorns probably come through sto-ries we read in our youth. The creature of these fables is very much with us in visual ways too. It is on the Royal coat of arms and often on pub signs. The physical form of the animal varies only a little in representation; usually an equine body, cloven hooves, often a goatee and always the long, tapering, spiral horn. Predominant in accounts of the unicorn are the practical quali-ties of the horn as an effective antidote and cure-all. It was trea-sured as a love potion and even today is spoken of as an aphrodisiac. The unicorn appears as a symbol of fertility, potency and trenchant virility. In the last of the great series of unicorn tapestries probably woven for the marriage of Frances I of France in 1514, the captured unicorn reposes, surrounded by flowers associated with sex, as a symbol of consummation. Clearly, so ancient, pervasive and consistent a myth must correspond with some deep-seated template bedded in the human unconscious: because the unicorn does not exist, it has been necessary to invent him. As a member of the human race, I have had no difficulty in locating one in my garden.

At this moment the unicorn sauntered by them, with his hands in his pockets. 'I had the best of it this time?' he said to the King, just glancing at him as he passed.

'A little – a little,' the King replied, rather nervously.

'You shouldn't have run him through with your horn, you know.'

'It didn't hurt him,' the Unicorn said carelessly, and he was going on, when his eye happened to fall upon Alice: he turned round instantly, and stood for some time looking at her with an air of the deepest disgust.

'What-is-this?' he said at last.

'This is a child!' Haigha replied eagerly, coming in front of Alice to introduce her, and spreading out both his hands towards her in an Anglo-Saxon attitude. 'We only found it today. It's as large as life, and twice as natural!'

'I always thought they were fabulous monsters!' said the Unicorn. 'Is it alive?'

'It can talk,' said Haigha solemnly.

The Unicorn looked dreamily at Alice, and said 'Talk, child.'

Alice could not help her lips curling up into a smile as she began: 'Do you know, I always thought Unicorns were fabulous monsters, too? I never saw one alive before!'

'Well, now that we have seen each other,' said the Unicorn, 'if you'll believe in me, I'll believe in you. Is that a bargain?'

'Yes, if you like.' said Alice.

LEWIS CARROL *Though the Looking Glass*

V

VIOLET

Scented out of all proportion with its size the sweet Violet, *Viola odorata*, has insinuated itself into the affections of western sensibility. It was a flower of Aphrodite and of her son Priapus, the deity of gardens and generation; these affiliations being prompted no doubt by its scent and manifested in the wreaths of violets worn by celebrants of the feast of Saturn dedicated to the god

Pan. Wearers of these headdresses may have benefited from the alleged property of the flowers to dispel the fumes of wine and prevent headache and dizziness. Gerard regarded violets benignly 'bicause the minde conceiveth a certaine pleasure and recreation by smelling and handling of these most odoriferous flowers... and the recreation of the minde which is taken heere by, cannot be but verie good and honest: for they admonish and stir up a man to that which is comely and honest.' The Violet was romantically associated with 'Caporal Violette', Napoleon, whose supporters used it as an emblem during his exile and who was welcomed back from Elba with posies of violets. When he died he was wearing a locket containing a lock of Josephine's hair and dried violets – her favourite flowers, always given to her by her husband on the anniversary of their wedding.

The single Garden Violet hath many round greene leaues, finely snipt or dented about the edges, standing vpon severall small stalkes, set at diuers places of the many creeping branches, which as they runne, doe here and there take roote in the ground, bearing theron many flowers generally at the ioynts of the leaves, which consist of fine small leaues, with a short round tayle or spurre behinde, of a perfect blew purple colour, and of a very sweet sent, it bringeth forth round seede vessels, standing likewise vpon their severall small stalkes, wherein is contained round white seed: but these heads rise not from where the flowers grew, as is all other plants that I know, but apart by themselves, and being sowne, will produce others like vnto it selfe, whereby there may be made a more speedy encrease to plant a Garden (as I have done) or any other place, than by slipping, as is the vsuall manner: the rootes spread both deepe and wide, taking strong hold in the ground.

JOHN PARKINSON *Paradisi in sole* 1629

VINCA

Culpepper distinguished between *Vinca minor* 'with the pale blue and… white flowers [which] grow in woods and orchards, by the Hedg-sides, in divers places of this land' and those, *Vinca major*, 'with purple flowers in Gardens onely'. Both appear to have been introduced early into Britain; Chaucer refers to it, along with the violet:

> There sprang the Violet all new
> And fresh Pervinke rich of hew.

The conjunction is additionally apt as both were associated with sex. According, again, to Culpepper 'Venus owns this Herb, and saith, that the Leaves eaten by Man and Wife together, cause Love between them'. An earlier recipe had prescribed Periwinkle powdered with earthworms to achieve the same effect. In Italy Vinca is sometimes known as *fiore di morte* 'flower of death' though it is unclear whether this derives from the custom of twining it into wreaths to place on the biers of dead children, or because garlands of it were hung on those who were to be executed – a custom practiced in medieval England too. In France, it is sometimes considered an emblem of friendship: perhaps in allusion to Rousseau's romantic remembrance of his friend of 30 years ago, Madame de Wavens, on seeing a Periwinkle in flower.

W

WISTERIA

Given the vigour with which *Wisteria sinensis* festoons itself on English walls one would not suspect that the plant's introduction was so fraught. Brought from China in 1816 one of the earliest specimens was taken on by Charles Hamden Turner who first kept it in his peach house at a temperature of 84° F, which together with depredations of vermin almost killed it. Its health improved when the temperature was reduced to 60°. Re-planted in vegetable mould, it was put out of doors in August and in September lost all its leaves. Overwintered in a cool greenhouse it began in March to show flower buds but put out no leaves until the end of the month when the flowers were nearly expanded. After judicious and progressive exposure to the open it got is roots down and since then, to the great delectation of succeeding generations, has never looked back. Wisteria was so named in 1818 after Dr Caspar Wistar of Philadelphia. Unfortunately his name was slightly mis-spelt and *wisteria* is set in stone; though some who think they know better sometimes try it on with *wistaria*.

WREN

The fagots cut in the winter from the hedges are here stacked up as high as the roof of a cottage and near by lies a help of ponderous logs waiting to be split for firewood. From exposure to the weather the bark of the fagot sticks has turned black, and rapidly decaying, and under it innumerable insects have made their homes.

For these, probably, the wrens visit the wood-pile continually: if in passing any one strikes the fagots with a stick, a wren will generally fly out the opposite side. They creep like mice in between the fagots – there are numerous interstices – and thus sometimes pass right through a corner of the stack.

RICHARD JEFFRIES *Wild Life in a Southern County*

Looking from a window at a bed of roses a few feet away, I discovered that the wren took as much pleasure in a dust bath as any bird. He would come to the loose soil and select a spot where the bed sloped towards the sun, and then wriggle about in the earth with immense enjoyment. Dusting himself, he would look like a miniature partridge with a round body not much bigger than a walnut. After dusting would come the luxurious sun-bath, when, with feathers raised and minute wings spread out and beak gaping, the little thing would lie motionless and panting; but at intervals of three or four seconds a joyful fit of shivering would seize him, and at last, the heat becoming too great, he would shake himself and skip away, looking like a brown young field vole scuttling into cover.

W. H. HUDSON *Hampshire Days*

X

Despite the abundance and, to those of us with small Latin and
less Greek, the obscurity of botanical nomenclature the Shorter
Oxford Dictionary lists only two plants whose names begin with
X. Neither is to be found in my garden; though, if I've got it
right, some of the bunches of dried flowers that hang from the

beams in the kitchen may well be of Xeranthemum. But rather than cheat by drawing what is in any case a rather undistinguished flower I have abstracted my X from the formality of a parterre enclosed by dwarf hedges of box, the shrub whose wood provides the xylographer, such as myself, with the surface on which to engrave. The boxwood used by engravers comes mostly from mediterranean countries but I have recently seen here in the village branches of box cut from a long-neglected hedge whose four and more inches diameter could, if only one had world enough and time to wait 10 years for it to season, furnish a lifetime's store of blocks.

...discoursing of the present fashion of gardens, to make them plain – that we have the best walks of Gravell in the world – France having none, nor Italy; and our green of our bowling-alleys is better then any they have. So our business here being ayre, this is the best way, only with a little mixture of Statues or pots, which may be hansome, and so filled with another pot of such or such, a flower or greene, as the season of the year will bear. And then for flowers, they are best seen in a little plat by themselves; besides, their borders spoil (the walks of) any other garden.

SAMUEL PEPYS   22 July 1666

Y

YARROW

A plant less to be cultivated than to be lived with. But useful perhaps in the context of a violent or accident-prone life-style. 'Wound-wert' and 'Knights Milfoil' testify to its efficacy in treating wounds. According to Gerard, it is the very plant with which

Achilles stanched the bleeding wounds of his soldiers; hence the generic name *Achillea*. Also known as 'Nosebleed', Parkinson tells us that 'if it be put into the nose, assuredly it will stay the bleeding of it'. On the other hand, if the leaf is rolled up and inserted in the nostrils it will cause bleeding from the nose and so relieve headaches. Confusing.

YELLOW-HAMMER

The female yellow-hammers, whose hues are not so brilliant as those of the male birds, seem as winter approaches to flock together, and roam the hedges and stubble fields in bevies. Where loads of corn have passed through gates the bushes often catch some straws, and the tops of the gateposts, being decayed and ragged, hold others. These are neglected while the seeds among the stubble, the charlock, and the autumn dandelion are plentiful and while the ears left by the gleaners may still be found. But in the shadowless winter days, hard and cold, each scattered straw is sought for.

A few days before the new year (1879) opened I saw a yellow-hammer attacking, in a very ingenious manner, a straw that hung pendant, the ear downwards, from the post of a windy gateway. She fluttered up from the ground, clung to the ear, and outspread her wings, keeping them rigid. The draught acted on the wings just as the breeze does on a paper kite, and there the bird remained supported without an effort while the ear was picked. Now and then the balance was lost, but she was soon up again, and again used the wind to maintain her position. The brilliant cockbirds return in the early spring, or at least appear to do so, for the habits of birds are sometimes quite local.

RICHARD JEFFRIES *The Amateur Poacher*

89

In the church yard of this village is a yew-tree, whose aspect bespeaks it to be of a great age: it seems to have seen several centuries, and is probably coeval with the church, and therefore may be deemed an antiquity: the body is squat, short, and thick, and measures twenty-three feet in the girth, supporting an head of suitable extent to it's bulk. This is a male tree, which in the spring sheds clouds of dust, and fills the atmosphere around with it's farina.

As far as we have been able to observe, the males of this species become much larger than the females; and it has so fallen out that most of the yew-trees in the church-yards of this neighbourhood are males; but this must have been matter of mere accident, since men, when they first planted yews, little dreamed that there were sexes in trees.

GILBERT WHITE *Natural History of Selbourne*

The churchyard of Selbourne is most beautifully situated. The land is good, all about it. The trees are luxuriant and prone to be lofty and large. I measured the yew-tree in the churchyard, and found the trunk to be, according to my measurement, twenty-three feet, eight inches, in circumference. The trunk is very short, as is generally the case with yew-trees; but the head spreads to a very great extent, and the whole tree, though probably several centuries old, appears to be in perfect health.

WILLIAM COBBETT *Rural Rides*

Z

ZINNIA

Like the sunflower, zinnias are native to Mexico where they were cultivated from an early date. By Montezuma's time zinnias had been highly developed, though for some reason seeds only reached Europe about the middle of the eighteenth century and it was not until the end of the century that *Z. elegans*, from which present day annual zinnias descend, was introduced. The zinnias with which we are familiar today testify to the skills of nineteenth-century nurserymen, mostly French, in creating natural flowers which, were they to be as artificial as they often appear, would be thought distinctly over the top. The plant was named in memory of J.G. Zinn, Professor of Botany and Natural History at Göttingen University who died in 1758. It is sometimes called 'Brazilian Marigold' which is misleading as it has no affiliation either with Brazil or the genus *Tagetes*.

ZUCCINI

It is surprising how recently the now ubiquitous zuccini has become a staple of English kitchens where, usually, it is called by its French name – courgette, (literally, little gourd). The Oxford Dictionary's first record of 'courgette' in an English cook book dates only from 1931 but the name and the vegetable itself is, like much else, largely the invention of Elizabeth David and her followers. In America, where the name zuccini, imported by generations of Italian immigrants, is preferred, the vegetable is perhaps less highly regarded. The International Zuccini Festival held every August in New Hampshire is said to be a way of celebrating the end of the annual glut. We in England may be more appreciative but have not yet cottoned on to the practice of French and Italian cooks of making the yellow trumpet blooms of the plant into little parcels of spiced or herbed rice ready for braising, steaming, or the sauté pan.

ACKNOWLEDGEMENTS

The author and publishers are grateful for permission to use:
Extract from Lord Emsworth and Others by P.G. Wodehouse reprinted by permission of the publishers Random House UK Ltd.
– *Diary* by Alan Bennett reprinted by permission of the London Review of Books 1996.
– from *The Tales of Peter Rabbit* by Beatrix Potter reprinted by permission of the publishers Frederick Warne & Co. Copyright Frederick Warne & Co 1902.
– *Autobiography* by Bertrand Russell reprinted by permission of the publishers Allen & Unwin.
– *L'Assommoir* by Emile Zola, translated by Leonard W. Tancock (Penguin Classics 1970). Copyright L.W. Tancock. 1970. Reprinted by permission of Penguin Books Ltd.

93